GREEK RECIPES

The Complete Step by Step Cookbook with Quick, Healthy and Nutritious Traditional Recipes from Greece

VIOLET HARVEY

TABLE OF CONTENTS

original author of this work can be in any fashion deemed liable for any hardship or damages that may befall them after undertaking information described herein.

Additionally, the information in the following pages is intended only for informational purposes and should thus be thought of as universal. As befitting its nature, it is presented without assurance regarding its prolonged validity or interim quality. Trademarks that are mentioned are done without written consent and can in no way be considered an endorsement from the trademark holder.

Adreana's Greek Pasta Salad

- 1 lb. rotini
- 1 lb. boneless skinless chicken breasts
- 3 stalks celery -- chopped
- red bell pepper -- chopped
- 1/4 oz black olives -- sliced
- oz feta cheese -- drained & crumbled
- green onions -- finely sliced
- 16 oz Italian salad dressing

Cook chicken in water to cover with 1 bay leaf. Bring to boil and cook for 30 min. or until juices run clear. Cool and remove skins.

Or, you can cook chicken in frying pan until cooked through. Cut into bite size pieces. Cook noodles and drain. Add all ingredients and mix well. I use only about half the bottle of dressing and then put the rest on the table if someone wants more.

Serve warm or cold.

Bastilla

- 1 lb. chicken breasts (or thighs)
- 1 md onion, chopped
- 3 c chicken stock, preferably-homemade
- 1/2 c fresh parsley, Chopped
- stick cinnamon (3 inches - long)
- 1/2 t ginger, Ground
- 1/8 t pepper
- 1/4 t saffron threads
- eggs

- 8 sheets phyllo dough, thawed
- T butter, melted
- 1 T granulated white sugar
- 1 t cinnamon
- 2/3 c chopped almonds, blanched
    - Powdered sugar, for garnish
    - Cinnamon, for garnish

Preheat oven to 425 F. In a large kettle add the chicken, stock, parsley, cinnamon stick, ginger, pepper and saffron. Bring to a boil over high heat. Cover, reduce heat and simmer until chicken is tender, about 30 to 45 minutes.

Lift chicken from stock and let stand until cool enough to handle. Remove and discard bones and skin. Shred the meat into bite size pieces.

Bring the broth to a boil over medium heat. Lightly beat eggs and pour slowly into the stock stirring until curds form, about 1 to 2 minutes. Pour mixture through a fine strainer placed over a bowl. Let stand until well drained. Reserve stock for soup or other uses. Discard the cinnamon stick.

Stack phyllo; keep covered to prevent drying out. Brush some of the butter on the bottom and sides of a 10-inch-deep pie pan. Overlap 6 sheets in the pan to cover bottom and extend 8 to 10 inches beyond edge. Brush phyllo with butter. Sprinkle sugar and second measure of cinnamon over phyllo. Top evenly with the chicken. Spread egg mixture over chicken, then sprinkle with almonds. Fold the edges of the phyllo over the filling and brush top with butter. Fold remaining 2 sheets of phyllo in half crosswise and place on pie. Tuck edges inside pan and brush top with butter.

Bake uncovered in a 425 oven for 20 minutes, or until golden brown. Shake pan to loosen pie. Hold an unrimmed baking sheet loosely over the top of the pie and invert pan. Lift off pan, return pie to the oven and bake until golden brown; about 10 minutes. Invert pie onto platter. Let stand 5 minutes. Sift powdered sugar generously over top and then decorate with crisscrossing lines of ground cinnamon.

Bear Steaks with Greek Seasonings

4 Servings

- 2 lb. bear steaks
- 1/2 c olive oil
- 1/2 c lemon juice
- 1 T garlic powder
- 1 t salt
- 1 t pepper
- 1 t combination of oregano
    - - marjoram, rosemary and/ o

Trim all visible fat from the bear as it turns rancid rapidly.

Whisk the other ingredients together until emulsified. Use the emulsion to marinate the meat for 2-3 hours, refrigerated. Longer marinading before cooking does not improve the meat as the remaining bear fat will go rancid despite refrigeration. Grill, broil or sauté the steaks until WELL DONE. Bear should always be thoroughly cooked as a trichinosis precaution. Serve immediately.

Do not try making a gravy from the marinade as it will usually have picked up a gamy taste from the bear meat.

Braised Lamb Shanks in Lemon-Dill Sauce

- 2 md onions, chopped (2 cups)
- 2 md carrots, chopped (1 cup)
- 2 cloves garlic
- 1 md leek
- 4 lg lamb shanks, about 1 pound, sawed crosswise into thirds
- 5 T olive oil
- 3 bay leaves

- 3 1/2 c fresh chicken stock or canned chicken broth
- 1 t salt
- 3 T fresh dill leaves, loosely packed
- 2 lemons,1/3 cup
- 2 eggs
- 1/2 t pepper, Fresh Ground

PREPARATION:

Peel onions, carrots, and garlic. Chop and put onions and carrots in a bowl with garlic. Rinse, trim, and chop leek, (using white portion and about 2 inches of the green), and add to the bowl. Pat shanks dry.

COOKING:

Adjust oven rack to middle position and heat oven to 350F. Heat 2 tablespoons of oil in a 5-quart Dutch oven until hot but not smoking.

Working in batches, sear lamb shanks over high heat until they are browned on all sides, about 7 minutes; set shanks aside.

Discard cooking fat and add remaining oil, vegetables and bay leaves. Cover and sauté over low heat, stirring occasionally, until vegetables are lightly colored, about 15 minutes. Return shanks and accumulated juices to the pot along with stock and 1 teaspoon salt.

Bring stock to a boil, reduce heat to low, and simmer, covered, for 45 minutes. Uncover and simmer until lamb is tender, 55-60 minutes. Remove shanks. Strain stock and return it to the pot. Bring to a boil, skimming it well, and reduce to 1 3/4 cups. (Can cover and refrigerate shanks in the stock for up to 2 days.)

SERVING:
If made ahead, heat shanks in foil in oven until hot. Bring stock to a boil. Mince dill. Squeeze 1/3 cup lemon juice into a medium bowl, whisk in eggs, and then slowly whisk in hot stock.

Stir in dill and 1/2 teaspoon pepper. Return the shanks to the pot, add the lemon-egg mixture and cook over low heat, gently stirring and shaking the pot, until shanks are warmed through and sauce has thickened slightly, about 5 minutes. Do not let sauce simmer or eggs may curdle.

Bulghur Pilaf

<u>4 Servings</u>

- 2 T butter (or oil)
- 1 sm onion, chopped
- 1/8 t salt
- 1/8 t turmeric
- 1/2 t thyme
- 1 c bulgur
- 1 3/4 c water and

- 1/4 c soy sauce (or tamari soy sauce)
- or 2 cups vegetable, beef,
    - -or
    - chicken stock
- 3/4 c sweet peas, Frozen
- 2 T carrots, Grated
- 2 T celery, Chopped
- 1 T raisins (optional), Chopped
- 2 T chopped parsley, (optional)

Satu onion in butter or oil or combination and add thyme and turmeric. Stir in bulghur and sauté while stirring for 3 minutes. Add liquid and salt and pepper. Cover and simmer for 25 minutes and stir in frozen peas, celery and grated carrot. Cover tightly and let sit off of the heat for 5 minutes. (Optional: Stir in chopped parsley and raisins). Serve.

Béchamel-Coated Fried Chicken

4 Servings

- 3 c chicken stock (or), Canned
    - -chicken broth
- 4 chicken breast halves
    - -skinned and, (1 1/2 pounds)
    - BECHAMEL COATING
- 5 T butter
- 6 T white flour
- 3/4 c milk
- 1/4 t thyme
    - Salt
    - White pepper, ground
- egg-beaten with 2
    - -tablespoons water
- 1 c dry bread crumbs
- quarts olive oil, for
    - -frying

TO PREPARE:

Bring chicken stock to boil in a large saucepan. Add chicken breasts; return stock to boil, cover, and simmer until chicken is cooked through, about 12 minutes. Remove chicken breast; reserve 3/4 cup of the chicken stock for the Béchamel Coating. Cool chicken breasts to room temperature.

Meanwhile, for the coating, heat butter in a small saucepan. Add flour; cook over low heat, stirring constantly until flour is incorporated into the butter, about 30 seconds. Continuing to stir constantly, gradually add milk and reserved 3/4 cup chicken stock. Simmer, still stirring constantly, until béchamel thickens, about 2 minutes. Stir in thyme and season with 1/4 teaspoon salt and 1/8 teaspoon white pepper or to taste; cool to room temperature. Dip each chicken breast in this béchamel, then refrigerate until béchamel is firm, about 1 hour. (Can be refrigerated overnight.)

TO COOK:

Heat oil in a Dutch oven or electric deep fryer to 365F. Dip both sides of each chicken breast into the egg-water mixture, then dredge in breadcrumbs. Dry chicken breasts, turning once, until golden brown, about 5 minutes. Drain chicken breasts on paper towels and serve.

Cabbage Salad

6 Servings

- 1 1/2 lb. green (or savoy cabbage),
  1 -medium
    - finely, Shredded
- 1 md onion, grated
- 2 T fresh parsley, Chopped
- 1/3 c olive oil, to taste
- 3 T wine vinegar, to taste
- 1 t sugar

  - salt and, Freshly Ground
  - -pepper, to taste
- green bell pepper, for
  - -garnish
  - seeded, deribbed, and cut in
    - thinner

In a large salad bowl, combine cabbage, onion, and parsley. In a small bowl whisk together oil, vinegar, sugar, salt, and ground pepper. Pour dressing over cabbage and toss until thoroughly coated. Arrange bell pepper rings on top. Cover and chill before serving.

Chiles & Garlic in Oil

<u>6 Servings</u>

- 2 lg red bell peppers
  - seeded and into 1/4", Sliced rings
  - or
- 3 fresh pimientos, with stems
- 6 fresh hot chiles
  - mixture of red, green, and
  - -yellow, with stems

- 3 long Italian chiles, with stems
- 6 sm onions, Boiling
- 20 lg garlic clove
- 1 lg onion
    - cut into 1/2" rings
    - fresh dill, * see note
- 2 c olive oil

Place all vegetables in a skillet (with a tight-fitting lid) large enough to hold them in a single layer. Lay dill on top and pour in enough olive oil to cover vegetables in pan. Put pan over moderate heat. When oil begins to simmer, reduce heat to lowest possible setting, turn vegetables over once, cover, and cook until boiling onions are quite soft (45 minutes to 1 hour).

If you have an electric stove, the lowest setting may not be low enough and you may need to use a heat diffuser. When vegetables are done, remove from heat, leave covered, and serve when cool.

Couscous

5 Servings

- 1 1/3 c couscous
- 2 c water
- 2 T butter
- 1 1/2 t salt

Add butter to boiling water, stir in couscous, cover and cook for three minutes. Turn off heat and let sit for 5 minutes, if fast cooking couscous. For regular, let sit for 10 - 15 minutes. Stir in salt and fluff before serving.

Cucumbers Stuffed with Feta

8 Servings

- 1/2 c feta cheese, Crumbled
- 1 T mayonnaise
- 2 dr Worcestershire sauce
- 4 sm cucumbers, chilled * see note
- 1 T minced fresh parsley, for garnish

In a small bowl combine cheese, mayonnaise, and Worcestershire sauce; mix well.

Fried Beer Batter-Coated Strawberries

4 Servings

APRICOT SAUCE

- 1/4 c apricot jam
- 1/2 T dark rum

FRIED BEER BATTER-COATED

-STRAWBERRIES

  - 2 quarts pure olive oil, for
    - frying
- 2/3 c white flour

- 2/3 c beer
- 1 1/2 T granulated sugar
- 16 large strawberries
- 2 T powdered sugar

TO PREPARE:

For the sauce, bring apricot jam, rum, and 1/4 cup water to boil in a small nonreactive saucepan. Simmer to blend flavors, about 4 minutes; cover and keep sauce warm.

TO COOK:

For the strawberries, heat oil in a Dutch oven or electric deep fryer to 365F. Mix flour, beer, and sugar in a small bowl. Dip each strawberry in this batter just before placing it in the hot oil. Working in batches to avoid overcrowding, fry strawberries until golden brown, 2 to 3 minutes.

Drain strawberries on paper towels.

TO SERVE:

Dust strawberries with confectioners' sugar and serve immediately with Apricot Sauce.

Fried Cinnamon Pastries with Honey Glaze

- 1/2 c vegetable oil
- 4 strips lemon zest 2 by-1/2-inch
- 2 sticks cinnamon,2 1/2-inch
- 1/2 c dry white wine
- 2 c white flour
- 1 c honey
- 3 T powdered sugar
- 1/4 t cinnamon, Ground

- 2 quarts olive oil, for-frying

TO PREPARE:

Cook vegetable oil and strips of lemon zest in a small saucepan over medium-high heat until lemon zest is dark brown, about 10 minutes.

Remove and discard zest. Cool vegetable oil slightly, then add cinnamon sticks.

Cover the pan with plastic wrap and let oil stand overnight. Then remove and discard cinnamon sticks.

Mix this cinnamon-flavored oil, the white wine, and the flour in a medium bowl; knead this dough in the bowl until it is smooth, about 2 minutes. Flatten the dough into a disk, wrap it in plastic wrap, and let it rest 30 minutes. On a lightly floured work surface, roll the dough into a 14- by 10-inch rectangle, about 1/8-inch thick. Cut this dough rectangle into seventy 2- by 1-inch strips; cover the dough strips with a kitchen towel and let them rest again for 30 minutes.

TO COOK:

Bring the honey and 1/4 cup water to boil in a small saucepan; simmer 15 minutes. Cover this honey mixture and keep it warm. Mix confectioners' sugar and cinnamon in a small bowl; set this cinnamon-sugar aside.

Meanwhile, heat the oil in a Dutch oven or electric deep fryer to 365F.

Working in batches to avoid overcrowding, fry the dough strips until they are golden brown, 2 to 3 minutes. Drain these fried pastries on paper towels. Dip each pastry in the honey mixture, then transfer pastry to a wire rack to allow excess honey to drain. Cool to room temperature, then dust pastries with the cinnamon-sugar. (Can be stored in an airtight container up to 3 days.)

Serves: 8 to 12

Fried Swordfish with Mediterranean Spices

4 Servings

- 1/2 c white wine vinegar
- 1/2 t paprika
- 1/2 t red pepper flakes, Dried
- 1/2 t oregano
- 1/2 t cumin, Ground
- 1/2 t thyme
- 3 md cloves garlic, minced
- bay leaf
    - Salt

- 1 1/2 lb. swordfish, cut in 1" pieces
- quarts olive oil, for frying
- 1/2 c white flour

TO PREPARE:

Mix first 8 ingredients plus 1/2 teaspoon salt in a medium nonreactive bowl. Add swordfish pieces; toss to coat. Cover and let stand at room temperature at least 1 hour. (Can be marinated up to 3 hours.)

TO COOK:

Heat oven to 200F. Heat oil in a Dutch oven or electric deep fryer to 365F. Transfer swordfish from marinade to a sieve. Drain swordfish; discard marinade. Pat swordfish pieces dry with paper towels, then dredge in flour.

Working in batches to avoid overcrowding, fry swordfish until golden brown, 2 to 3 minutes. Drain swordfish pieces on paper towel; transfer to a heatproof platter and keep them warm in the oven until ready to serve. (Can be kept warm in the oven up to 1/2 hour.)

Ginza

4 Servings

- 3 eggs
- 3/4 c milk
- 1/8 t salt
- 1/2 t granulated white sugar
- 1 1/2 c white wheat flour
- 2 T brown sugar, sprinkle over
    - mixture before serving

Mix all ingredients in a blender and pour into 1/4 inch of oil on medium heat setting in a cast iron pan. Using two forks crisscross through the mixture until golden brown.

Greek Easter Lamb

8 Servings

- 5 lb. leg of lamb, or kid
- 1 t salt
- 2 T fresh oregano leaves
    - or
- 2 t oregano leaves, Dried
- 2 T fresh basil leaves
    - or

- 2 t basil leaves, Dried
- 2 T fresh mint leaves
    - or
- 2 t mint leaves, Dried
- 3 T fresh rosemary leaves
    - or
- 1 1/2 T rosemary, Dried
- 1 T fresh thyme leaves
    - or
- 1 t thyme leaves, Dried
- 4 lg garlic cloves
    - crushed, peeled, and
    - -coarsely mince
- 1 c olive oil
- 6 T fresh lemon juice

Two to four hours before roasting, remove meat from refrigerator.

Trim all outside fat and prominent sinews. In a food processor, blender, or electric mincer puree together salt, oregano, basil, mint, rosemary, thyme, and garlic. (Add 1 or 2 spoonful olive oil if needed.) If no electric appliance is available, mince herbs and seasonings and pound in a mortar. Rub herb mixture on lamb. Stir together olive oil and lemon juice and paint some generously on meat, reserving remainder. Let meat stand at least 2 hours. Preheat oven to 475 degrees. Place leg on rack in roasting pan in center of oven. Lower heat to 350 degrees. Brush meat with reserved oil mixture every 10 minutes. Roast until internal temperature at thickest part registers 135 degrees on an instant-read meat thermometer (20 minutes per pound) for rare, 150 degrees for medium, and 165 degrees for medium well-done. Let meat rest before slicing across grain.

Greek Meatballs with Mint

<u>12 Servings</u>

- 1 lb. lean beef, Ground
- 1 lb. veal (or pork)
- 2 eggs
- 1 lg onion, grated
- 1 T fresh mint, Minced
- 1 T oregano
- 2 T fresh parsley, Minced
- 2 cloves garlic, minced
- 1 T tomato paste
    - diluted in 1 tablespoon

- -water
- 2 T olive oil
    - plus, olive oil for pan
    - -frying
- 12 whole salted wheat crackers
    - and squeezed, Soaked in Water
        - dry
- 1/2 c dry white wine
    - salt and, Freshly Ground
    - -pepper, to taste
    - flour, for dusting

Place meat in a large mixing bowl. Break in eggs and mix well. Add
onion, mint, oregano, parsley, garlic, diluted tomato paste, the 2 tablespoons oil, crackers, wine, salt, and pepper. Knead until well mixed and smooth. On a lightly floured board, shape meat mixture into 12 balls. With your palms, flatten balls into patties, then dust patties lightly with flour. In a large skillet over medium heat, warm the remaining oil. Fry patties, turning once, until browned on both sides, 2 to 3 minutes per side or until done to your liking.

Greek Salad

4 Servings

- 2 green bell peppers

  washed, seeded, and cut into 1" cub
- cucumber

  peeled and cut into 1" Cubes
- tomatoes

  washed and cut into 1" Cubes
- stalks celery

- washed & diagonally, Sliced into 1/2
- 1/4 lb. feta cheese, cut into 1/2" cubes
- 1/2 red onion, diced
- 1/2 t kosher salt
- pepper, Freshly Ground
- T vinegar
- 1/4 c oil
- 1/2 t oregano
- 1 T fresh basil, minced

In a 2-quart bowl, mix peppers, cucumber, tomatoes, celery, feta cheese, and red onion. Season with salt, pepper, vinegar, oil, oregano, and basil.

Greek Stifado With Feta Cheese Crust

- 2 T olive oil
- 3 T butter
- 3 lb. lean beef stew meat, cut into 1" Cubes
- 1 md onion, minced
- 1/2 c tomato paste
- 1/2 c dry white wine
- 1/4 c red wine vinegar
- 3/4 c water
- 2 T garlic, Minced

- bay leaf
- 1 t oregano leaves, Dried-crumbled
- 1 t cinnamon, Ground
- 1/2 t cumin, Ground
- 1/2 t sugar
- 1/4 t cayenne pepper, or to taste
    - salt and, Freshly Ground black pepper, to taste
- 16 sm white boiling onions, peeled
- 1/2 c pine nuts
- 1/2 lb. feta cheese, crumbled or grated
- 1/2 c parsley, Minced
    - hot-pepper sauce, optional

In a large, heavy skillet, heat oil and butter over moderate heat.
Raise heat to high and brown meat, one third at a time, removing meat to a large, heavy casserole (preferably with an enamel or porcelain coating) as it browns.

Add minced onion to skillet, sauté just until wilted, and spoon into casserole. Add tomato paste, wine, vinegar, the water, garlic, bay leaf, oregano, cinnamon, cumin, and sugar to the casserole.

Stir well and add cayenne, salt, and pepper, to taste. Bring just to a boil, cover tightly, lower heat, and simmer 1 hour.

Add white boiling onions and simmer, covered, until meat is very tender (about 1 hour longer). Degrease stew if necessary and carefully correct seasonings; stir in nuts. Sprinkle feta cheese over stew, pushing it gently into top of liquid with a wooden spoon. Cover and simmer to melt cheese (about 5 minutes longer).

Sprinkle parsley on top and serve stew in deep soup bowls, making sure that everyone gets some nuts and cheese, but leaving some room in each bowl for rice to be added. Have hot-pepper sauce on hand, to be added as desired.

Greek Walnut Cake

<u>36 Servings</u>

   - Cinnamon Sugar Syrup, see recipe
- 1 c unsalted butter, softened
   - plus, butter for baking dish
- 1 c sugar
- 6 eggs
- 1 c flour, sifted
- 1 c farina
- 2 1/2 t baking powder
- 1 t cinnamon, Ground

- 1 t orange zest, Freshly Grated
- 1 c finely walnuts, Chopped

Prepare syrup and set aside to cool. Preheat oven to 350 degrees. In a large mixing bowl, cream together the 1 cup butter and sugar with a wooden spoon until light and fluffy. Add eggs, one at a time, beating continuously. Beat in flour, farina, baking powder, cinnamon, and orange zest. Mix in walnuts. Butter a 9 by 13-inch baking dish and pour batter into it. Bake until a knife blade inserted in center comes out clean (about 30 minutes). Remove cake from oven and immediately pour cooled syrup evenly over top. Cool to room temperature.

Green Bean Salad With Feta-Walnut Mimosa

VINAIGRETTE

- scallion
- 4 t white wine vinegar
- 1/4 c walnut oil (or vegetable oil)
    - Salt
    - black pepper, Fresh Ground

SALAD

- 1 1/4 oz walnuts-about 1/3 cup, Halved
- 1 1/2 lb. green beans
- 2 eggs
- 2 1/2 oz feta cheese about 1/2 cup, Crumbled

PREPARATION:

For the vinaigrette, mince the scallion. In a small bowl, mix the vinegar, oil, and scallion. Season to taste with salt and pepper.

Heat oven to 350F. Put walnuts in a cake pan and toast, stirring once or twice, until lightly browned, about 7 minutes. Cool and then chop finely.

Cook beans in a large pot of boiling, salted water until crisp-tender, about 4 minutes. Rinse under cold running water and drain thoroughly.
Gently pat dry.

Put eggs in a saucepan, cover with water, and bring to a simmer. Cover, remove saucepan from heat, let stand for 20 minutes, drain. Cool eggs, separate whites from yolks, and chop separately into fine dice.

Recipe can be made to this point several hours ahead.

SERVING:
Arrange beans on a round serving platter in a circular fashion with the ends meeting in the center. Whisk vinaigrette and spoon it evenly over the beans. Crumble the feta cheese and sprinkle it in the center of the plate. Sprinkle chopped walnuts in a circle around the cheese. Sprinkle chopped egg yolks in a circle around walnuts; then sprinkle chopped egg whites in a circle around the yolks, covering all but the outer ends of the beans. Serve at room temperature.

Grilled/Chilled Tuna with Tangerines

MARINADE

- 1 T tamari soy sauce
- 1/4 c olive oil
- 1 T fresh fennel leaf, Chopped
- 2 t fresh celery leaves
- 1/2 t fresh thyme, Chopped
- 1 sm bay leaf, broken
- 2 t tangerine zest, Grated
    - Black pepper

FISH

- 1 lb. fresh tuna center-cut into four 4 oz. steaks,1 inch thick
- 4 tangerines
- 16 sprigs fresh fennel leaf

TANGERINE AND FENNEL VINAIGRETTE

- 3 T balsamic vinegar
- 1 t Dijon mustard
- 1/2 c light olive oil
- 1/2 t tangerine zest, Grated
- 2 T fresh fennel leaf
    - Salt (or black pepper)

1. For the marinade, combine all marinade ingredients in a nonreactive bowl.

2. Put tuna steaks into marinade and refrigerate 30 min, turning occasionally.

3. Break 2 of the tangerines into sections. Squeeze the remaining 2 tangerines, pour juice over sectioned tangerines, and set aside.

4. Heat grill. Add mesquite or hickory chips for additional flavor.

5. Remove tuna steaks from marinade and grill over hot fire until fish is just springy to the touch, 1 to 2 minutes per side. Tuna should be rare to medium rare.

6. Divide each tuna steak into 3 to 4 slices, cutting against the grain. Drain tangerine sections and reserve juice. Arrange tuna slices with drained tangerine sections and fennel sprigs in fan shape on individual plates, cover, and chill. Reduce tangerine juice by one-fourth over medium-high heat and use to make vinaigrette.

7. For the vinaigrette, combine vinegar, reduced tangerine juice, and mustard in a nonreactive bowl. Whisk in oil and season with tangerine zest, chopped fennel leaves, and salt and pepper to taste.

8. Drizzle dressing over arranged salad plates just before serving.

Lamb and White Bean Ragout

- 1 1/2 c Great Northern beans, Dried-about 12 oz.
- 3 t Salt
- 6 lb. lamb shoulder (6-7 pounds) trimmed and boned
- 8 cloves garlic
- 1 c red wine

- 1/3 c red wine vinegar
- 1/2 c olive oil
- 1 t thyme, Dried
- 1 t marjoram, Dried
- 1 t basil, Dried
- 2 bay leaves
- 2 md onions
- 5 carrots
- 35 oz (1 can) Italian plum tomatoes
- 1/4 c white flour
- 2 c beef stock (or beef), Canned
- 1/2 c Niçoise olives
- 1/2 c fresh parsley leaves-stemmed, firmly packed
- 1/2 t black pepper, Fresh Ground

PREPARATION:

Rinse, pick over beans, and put them in bowl with cold water to cover by 3 inches. Let stand for 24 hours; drain. Or, put beans in a 5-quart soup kettle or Dutch oven with water to cover, bring to a boil, cover, remove from heat, and let stand 1 hour; drain. Return drained beans to soup kettle, and add cold water to cover by 3 inches. Bring to a boil, turn heat to low and simmer, partially covered, until the beans are almost tender, about 1 hour. Stir in 1 teaspoon of salt and continue cooking until the beans are tender, 15 to 20 minutes. Drain and set aside. Cut lamb into 1 1/2-inch cubes. Peel and crush the garlic and put it in a non-reactive bowl with the wine, vinegar, 3 tablespoons oil, thyme, marjoram, basil, and bay leaves. Add the lamb and marinate for at least two hours. (Can cover and refrigerate the beans and meat separately overnight.) Peel and chop the onions (2 cups). Peel and cut carrots into 1/2-inch slices. Drain the tomatoes and set vegetables aside separately.

COOKING:

Adjust oven rack to low position and heat oven to 350F. Remove the lamb
from the marinade and pat dry on paper toweling. Heat 3 tablespoons of

the oil in the Dutch oven or soup kettle until hot but not smoking. Working in batches, sear the lamb over high heat until well browned, adding additional oil as needed, and removing lamb to a bowl with a slotted spoon or until tender, about 10 minutes. Stir in the flour and cook 3 minutes. Whisk in the reserved marinade and beef stock. Stir in the tomatoes and 2 teaspoons salt, and bring to a boil. Return meat to the kettle with any accumulated juices, cover with foil and the lid and bake 1 hour. Skim, stir in the carrots and bake, uncovered, for 30 minutes. Stir in the beans and bake until stew thickens slightly, about 15 minutes. Rinse and drain the olives. Mince the parsley. Stir in olives and parsley and season with 1/2 teaspoon pepper and salt to taste.

Lima Bean Plaki

8 Servings

- 1 lb. dried lima beans, * see note
- 3/4 c olive oil
- onion, finely chopped
- cloves garlic, minced
- carrots, finely chopped
- stalk celery, finely chopped

- 1/2 c fresh parsley, Chopped
- T chopped fresh dill, crushed
- 1 t dried fines herbs, crushed
- T fresh lemon juice
- 16 oz plum tomatoes, with their liquid
- 2 c chicken stock
    - salt and, Freshly Ground
    - -pepper, to taste
- 2 c water

Place beans in a saucepan with water to cover, bring to a boil, and parboil 25 minutes. Drain and set aside. In a Dutch oven over medium-high heat, warm oil. Add onion, garlic, carrots, celery, and parsley; sauté until onion is translucent (about 5 minutes). Add dill, fines herbs, lemon juice, tomatoes, stock, salt, and pepper. Bring to a boil, reduce heat, and simmer 20 minutes. Add drained beans and the water; simmer until beans are tender (about 25 minutes).

Pork Chops with Apples in Cider Sauce

4 Servings

- 2 T vegetable oil, approximately to film skillet
- 4 loin pork chops,1/2 lb. each
- 2 T butter, Unsalted
- 2 md red onions
    - and cut into 1/4-inch, Peeled Slices

- 1 T garlic, Minced
- 2 lg sweet apples, cut into 1/2" slices
    - quartered, peeled, and cored
- 1 T fresh sage
    - or
- 1 t sage, Dried
- 1/2 t dried thyme leaves, crumbled
- 3/4 c unsweetened apple juice
- 1/2 c dry white wine
    - salt and, Freshly Ground
    - -pepper, to taste

Film a large, heavy skillet with oil and heat over a high flame
until oil is fragrant. Pat pork chops dry, quickly brown on both sides in skillet, and remove to a plate. Lower heat to medium and melt butter in skillet. Add onions and sauté, stirring occasionally, until softened. Add garlic and sauté until translucent (1 minute longer).

Add apples and turn in butter just until completely coated. Return pork chops to skillet, sprinkle with sage and thyme, and add cider and wine. Bring liquid to a simmer and cook over fairly low heat until chops are cooked through (20 minutes).

With a slotted spatula remove chops and apple mixture from skillet and keep warm. Reduce cooking liquid at a full boil over high flame, stirring constantly, until it has thickened to the consistency of light syrup.

Add salt and pepper to taste, pour liquid over chops and apples, and serve hot.

Rice Pilaf

4 Servings

- 2 T butter (or oil)
- 1 sm onion, chopped
  - or 1/2 cup scallions, Chopped
- 1/8 t salt
- 1/8 t turmeric
- 1/2 t thyme
- 1 c brown rice (or rice)
- 2 1/2 c water and
- 1/2 c soy sauce (or tamari soy)
  - -sauce
  - or 3 cups vegetable, beef
  - or chicken stock
- 3/4 c sweet peas, Frozen
- 1/4 c carrots, Grated
- 1/4 c celery, Chopped
- 1/4 c green bell peppers, Minced (optional)
- 1 T raisins (optional), Chopped
- 2 T chopped parsley, (optional)

Sauté onion (if using scallions skip this step) in butter or oil or combination and add thyme and turmeric. Stir in rice and sauté while stirring for 3 minutes. Add liquid and salt and pepper. Cover and simmer for 35 minutes (less for white, hulled rice). Stir in frozen peas, celery and grated carrot. Cover tightly and let sit off of the heat for 7 minutes. Add scallion and, if using, chopped parsley, green pepper and raisins. Serve.

Roasted Chicken with Lemon-Parsley Sauce

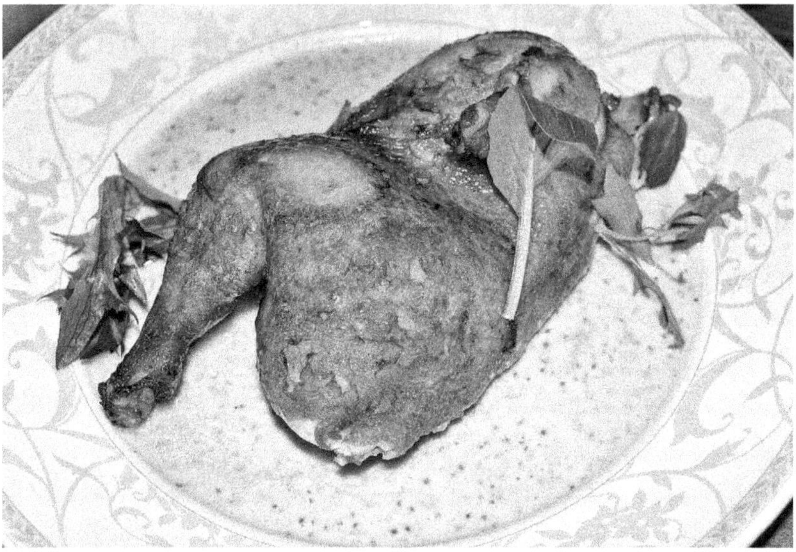

4 Servings

- lemon
- 4 T butter
- whole chicken breasts split
    - Salt
    - black pepper, Fresh Ground
- 1/3 c parsley, Chopped

COOKING AND SERVING:

Heat oven to 450F. Squeeze 1/4 cup lemon juice. Melt the butter in a small saucepan or in the microwave. Sprinkle chicken with salt and pepper. Put chicken in a baking dish skin side up and drizzle with half of the butter.

Bake until skin is crisp and golden brown and juices run clear, about 25 to 30 minutes. Put chicken on a serving platter and keep warm.

Stir the lemon juice and remaining butter into pan juices, scraping the pan with a wooden spoon to deglaze. Add the parsley and season to taste with salt and pepper. Pour sauce over chicken and serve immediately.

Stuffed Grape Leaves

- 1/4 c currants, Dried
- 1 c dry white wine
- 12 T olive oil
- 6 green onions and green tops- finely, Chopped
- 1 T fresh parsley, Minced
- 3/4 c long-grain white rice
- 1 T fresh dill, Minced
- 1/4 c pine nuts
    - salt and, Freshly Ground pepper, to taste

- 16 oz grape leaves preserved in brine water, Boiling
- 6 T fresh lemon juice
- 2 c beef stock
    - Lemon wedges & chilled plain
        - yogurt, for accompaniment

In a small bowl combine currants and wine; set aside. In a small
skillet over medium heat, warm 2 tablespoons of the oil. Add onions and parsley and sauté until onions are translucent (about 5 minutes). Add rice, dill, pine nuts, currants and wine, salt, and pepper; stir to mix, cover, and simmer until liquid is absorbed (about 10 minutes).

Remove from heat and cool. Remove grape leaves from jar and immerse in boiling water about 30 seconds; drain and rinse under cold water. Cut off and discard tough stems. Pat leaves dry with paper towels, then place shiny side down on a flat surface.

Place a rounded teaspoon of the rice mixture on center of each leaf.

Fold base end of leaf over filling to cover; fold in sides of leaf,
overlapping them, then roll up carefully to form a sealed cylinder about 2 inches long. Repeat with remaining leaves.

In bottom of a Dutch oven or other heavy, broad-bottomed pan, arrange a layer of stuffed leaves, seam side down, close together. Sprinkle with some of the lemon juice and 2 tablespoons of the olive oil. Repeat, making as many layers as necessary to accommodate all of the stuffed leaves; sprinkle each layer with lemon juice and olive oil. Pour in beef stock and the remaining olive oil, being careful not to disturb layers. Place a heavy plate on top to weight down stuffed leaves. Cover and simmer over very low heat until rice is tender (about 40 minutes). To test, open one of the packets. Remove from heat and lift stuffed leaves out with a slotted utensil.

Whole Stuffed Leg of Lamb

Stuffing

- 2 c al dente bulgur, Cooked
- 6 cloves garlic, minced
- 1 lg onion, chopped
- 2 stalks celery, chopped
- 1 lg bell pepper, seeded and-chopped
- 6 sm fresh hot chilies, seeded and Minced
- 1/3 c fresh parsley, Minced
- 1 T fresh dill weed, Minced or 1 t dill weed, Dried

- 1/2 t cumin, Ground
- 6 T fresh lemon juice
- 1 t lemon peel, Grated
- bay leaf
- 1/3 c pine nuts
- 1/3 c currants
- eggs, lightly beaten
- 1 t sugar
    - salt and, Coarsely Ground black pepper to taste
- 8 lb. leg of lamb, * see note
    - Marinade
- fresh lemon juice
- 1/4 c sugar
- 1/4 c olive oil
- 1 T fresh dill weed, Minced or 1 t dill weed, Dried
- cloves garlic, finely minced
- 1/4 t cayenne
- bay leaf
- 1 t dry mustard
- 1/2 t mixed dried herbs, Italian-seasoning
- 1/2 T paprika
    - Salt and black, Fresh Ground pepper
- 1/2 c beef broth

- Lettuce leaves, tomato-wedges, and lemon slices (optional)

Combine all of the ingredients for the stuffing and pack them firmly into the leg of lamb. Truss shut with bamboo or metal skewers. Mix all the ingredients for the marinade together exceedingly well. Put the stuffed leg of lamb in a deep dish, pour the marinade over, and rub it into the meat on all sides.

Refrigerate overnight, turning and rubbing several times. To bake, place the lamb in a roasting pan with a tight-fitting lid. Mix the broth with the remaining marinade and pour over the leg of lamb.

Bake at 350 degrees for 1 1/2 hours or until the meat is exceedingly tender.
Remove the lid during the last 20 minutes and turn the heat to 400 degrees to brown.

Authentic Greek Moussaka

8-10 Servings

Ingredients

- 3 potatoes
- 5-6 tablespoon(s) olive oil
- 1 onion
- 2 zucchinis, medium
- 2 eggplants
- thyme
- salt

- pepper

For the ground meat

- 1 onion
- 2 tablespoon(s) olive oil, for sautéing
- 1 clove(s) of garlic
- 3 pinches granulated sugar
- 1/2 teaspoon(s) nutmeg
- 1 level teaspoon(s) cinnamon
- 1 tablespoon(s) tomato paste
- 500 g ground beef
- 400 g canned tomatoes
- salt
- pepper

For the béchamel sauce

- 1 onion
- 2 tablespoon(s) olive oil, for sautéing
- 1 clove(s) of garlic
- 3 pinches granulated sugar
- 1/2 teaspoon(s) nutmeg
- 1 level teaspoon(s) cinnamon
- 1 tablespoon(s) tomato paste
- 500 g ground beef
- 400 g canned tomatoes

- salt
- pepper

Combine all of the ingredients for the stuffing and pack them firmly into the leg of lamb. Truss shut with bamboo or metal skewers. Mix all the ingredients for the marinade together exceedingly well. Put the stuffed leg of lamb in a deep dish, pour the marinade over, and rub it into the meat on all sides. Refrigerate overnight, turning and rubbing several times. To bake, place the lamb in a roasting pan with a tight-fitting lid. Mix the broth with the remaining marinade and pour over the leg of lamb. Bake at 350 degrees for 1 1/2 hours or until the meat is exceedingly tender. Remove the lid during the last 20 minutes and turn the heat to 400 degrees to brown.

CPSIA information can be obtained
at www.ICGtesting.com
Printed in the USA
LVHW080143230521
688251LV00002B/113

9 781802 665581